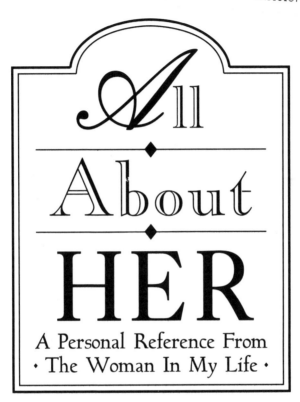

All About HER

A Personal Reference From
· The Woman In My Life ·

Created by Beverly Clark and Marcella L. Jaegle

All About Her

A Personal Reference Book
From the Woman in My Life

You will know exactly what to do for her
to make her feel special
without having to ask!
Now when she says, "Remember me..."

Created by Beverly Clark and Marcella L. Jaegle
Wilshire Publications

Dedication

May this book inspire romance, imagination and
resourcefulness...qualities we know all men possess, but which
may lay dormant in them.

—Beverly Clark

For my husband, Fred, who inspired this book. Through him I
saw how difficult it was to juggle life and me too.

—Marcella L. Jaegle

I dedicate this to you

Getting Started

T here are so many things to remember about a woman to make her feel special. Life's complications often interfere with memory recall. Although this is logical, emotions are not so easily convinced. This book may not hold all the answers for you or your relationship, but can be a big help! Ask for what you want, and what you need. A healthy relationship is a learning process that can be enjoyed together.

Present this book to your partner when you have the time to look through it together. Allow your partner to fill this book with her own intimate thoughts, at her own pace, privately. Both of you should know that it is not necessary to answer all the questions, but always answer honestly. It is all right to answer "no," or "never, please do not!"

Refer to the completed book whenever you feel the need for direction or insight. Understand that people change with time and it might be necessary for your partner to use the note pages to update this book. The note pages are included for your use as well. Use them to store your thoughts and ideas about a particular issue or future plan.

This book was designed to help you create wonderful moments in your relationship. A thoughtful word, gesture or gift is a welcome oasis in the desert of everyday life. Nurturing a relationship is important, and your efforts will be felt, recognized and appreciated.

"There might be much on my mind,
There might be words I can't find,
But my heart is always with you."
— Lisa Marie Nelson

"The only true gift
is a portion of yourself"

— *Ralph Waldo Emerson*

Traditional Holidays

December 31...New Year's Eve

February 14 ....Valentine's Day

March 17...St. Patrick's Day

March or April...Passover and Easter

May 1...May Day

Second Sunday in May ....Mother's Day

Third Sunday in June ....Father's Day

July 4...Fourth of July

First Monday in September ....Labor Day

October 31 ....Halloween

Last Thursday in November ....Thanksgiving

November or December..Hanukkah

December 25...Christmas

Anniversaries

First Year ....Paper
Second ....Cotton
Third ....Leather
Fourth ....Books
Fifth ....Wood or Clocks
Sixth ....Iron
Seventh ....Copper, Bronze or Brass
Eighth...Electrical Appliances
Ninth ....Pottery
Tenth ....Tin
Eleventh...Steel
Twelfth..Silk or Linen
Thirteenth...Lace
Fourteenth ....Ivory
Fifteenth ....Crystal
Twentieth..China
Twenty-fifth ....Silver
Thirtieth...Pearl
Thirty-fifth...Coral
Fortieth ....Ruby
Forty-fifth...Sapphire
Fiftieth ....Gold
Sixtieth..Diamond
Seventy-fifth ....Platinum

Who am I?

Name given at birth _____

I like to be called _____

_____

Birthday _____

Birthstone _____

Astrological sign _____

Flower _____

Favorite things:

color _____ flower _____

gem _____ place _____

Hobbies: _____

_____

_____

_____

Important Information About Me

Driver's License # _____

Social Security # _____

Blood type_____

Allergies (food & drug) _____

_____

About My Health_____

_____

_____

Medical Information _____

_____

_____

Medication you should know about _____

_____

_____

_____

About My Family

Parents' names _____

_____

Mother's maiden name _____

My father's family is originally from _____

_____

My mother's family is originally from _____

_____

Siblings _____

_____

_____

_____

Other close relatives_____

_____

_____

_____

Notes

There is but one genuine love-potion — consideration.
— *Meander*

Traditions in My Life

I feel that traditions _____

_____

_____

Here are a few traditions I hold dear _____

_____

_____

Childhood celebrations _____

_____

_____

Family occasions _____

_____

_____

Holiday rituals _____

_____

_____

Notes

"Among those whom I like I can find no common denomination, but
among those whom I love, I can; all of them make me laugh."
— *W.H. Auden*

People in My Life

Besides you, I...

most admire _____

am influenced by _____

most want to be like _____

feel it is easiest to talk to _____

trust _____

have fun with _____

Who would I like to invite to my own party?

_____

_____

_____

The three people in my life that might know almost everything about me there is to know

_____

_____

_____

Professionals in My Life

	Name	Phone #
Doctors	_____	_____
	_____	_____
	_____	_____
	_____	_____
	_____	_____
Dentist	_____	_____
Lawyer	_____	_____
Accountant	_____	_____
Others	_____	_____
	_____	_____
	_____	_____
	_____	_____

Days to Remember Me

My favorite major holiday(s) _____

_____

_____

_____

Favorite minor holidays _____

_____

_____

_____

My special days

Date _____ *Occasion* _____

Date _____ *Occasion* _____

Date _____ *Occasion* _____

Ways you can remember me

_____

_____

_____

_____

Do Me a Favor

When I'm happy _____

_____

_____

When I want to celebrate _____

_____

_____

When I want attention _____

_____

_____

Around the house _____

_____

When life gets too serious _____

_____

When I'm feeling low _____

_____

More Favors

When I'm fatigued _____

_____

_____

When I am sick _____

_____

_____

When I am frustrated_____

_____

_____

When I am angry with you _____

_____

_____

When I am mad at the world _____

_____

_____

Notes

_____

_____

_____

_____

_____

_____

_____

_____

_____

_____

_____

_____

_____

_____

_____

_____

_____

_____

"Who loves well, forgets slowly."
— *French Proverb*

I Like

Actor(s) _____

_____

_____

_____

Actress(es) _____

_____

_____

_____

Movies to rent (title or type) _____

_____

_____

_____

Movies to go see _____

_____

_____

All-time favorite movie_____

I Like

To read _____

_____

_____

_____

All-time favorite book _____

Authors I enjoy _____

_____

_____

_____

_____

Favorite poem _____

Favorite library _____

Favorite bookstore _____

Favorite magazine _____

I Like

Singer(s) _____

_____

_____

_____

_____

Song(s) _____

_____

_____

_____

Radio station _____

Entertainer _____

_____

_____

Playing the game(s) of _____

_____

_____

Notes

_____

_____

_____

_____

_____

_____

_____

_____

_____

_____

_____

_____

_____

_____

_____

"I like not only to be loved,
but to be told I am loved."
— *George Elliot*

Things I Like

To do _____

_____

_____

To see _____

_____

_____

To hear _____

_____

_____

To smell _____

_____

_____

To taste _____

_____

_____

Notes

_____

_____

_____

_____

_____

_____

_____

_____

_____

_____

_____

_____

_____

_____

"In the game of love there is no sport.
If it is played well, everyone wins."
— *Marci Jaegle*

Sports

I like to watch _____

_____

_____

I like to play _____

_____

_____

I enjoy competitive _____

_____

_____

I would like to have more time to _____

_____

_____

I would like to learn _____

_____

_____

Notes

_____

_____

_____

_____

_____

_____

_____

_____

_____

_____

_____

_____

_____

_____

_____

_____

_____

_____

"To love is to choose."
— *Joseph Roux*

Activities I enjoy

On a rainy day _____

_____

_____

When the sun shines bright _____

_____

_____

I feel best when I wear _____

_____

_____

I like to collect _____

_____

_____

I've been looking for _____

_____

_____

Notes

_____

_____

_____

_____

_____

_____

_____

_____

_____

_____

_____

_____

_____

_____

_____

_____

_____

"We don't love qualities, we love a person;
sometimes by reason of their defects as well as their qualities."
— *Jacques Maritain*

Just my size!

Blouse _____   Dress _____

Pants _____   Jeans _____

T-shirt _____Skirt _____

Suit _____Slip _____

Bra_____ Panties _____ Panty style_____

Pajamas _____Robe _____

Shoe _____ Necklace style _____

Ring size _____ Wrist size _____

Earring preference _____

Notes:

_____

_____

_____

_____

_____

Notes

_____

_____

_____

_____

_____

_____

_____

_____

_____

_____

_____

_____

_____

_____

_____

_____

_____

"Love is, above all, the gift of one's self."
— *Jean Anouilh*

Where I like to shop

My favorite clothing store _____

_____

phone # _____

address _____

My favorite lingerie store _____

_____

phone # _____

address _____

My favorite shoe store _____

_____

phone # _____

address _____

My favorite specialty shop _____

_____

phone # _____

address _____

Notes

_____

_____

_____

_____

_____

_____

_____

_____

_____

_____

_____

_____

_____

_____

_____

_____

"I once had been lost, but when I met you I was found.
You came into my life and turned my world around."
— *Lisa Marie Nelson*

You Are on the Road

If you are traveling and want to get me a "little something" and have no time for a real store or exploration...

I always enjoy receiving something from:

An airport gift shop _____

A roadside stand _____

A drug store _____

A hotel gift shop _____

Duty-free shop _____

Other _____

_____

_____

_____

Notes

_____

_____

_____

_____

_____

_____

_____

_____

_____

_____

_____

_____

_____

_____

_____

_____

_____

_____

_____

_____

_____

"You will do foolish things, but do them with enthusiasm."
— _Collette_

You Can Remember Me,
and it Won't Cost a Dime

There are things that you can do for me that will make me feel special.

_____

_____

_____

_____

_____

_____

_____

_____

_____

_____

_____

_____

_____

_____

Notes

"Kissing your hand may make you feel good,
but a diamond and sapphire bracelet lasts forever."
—*Anita Loos*

Break the Bank!

So you want to spend some money on me?
Here are a few gifts I dream about:

I have never owned a brand new_____

_____

_____

_____

I dream about buying _____

_____

_____

_____

Some day I want_____

_____

_____

_____

Some day, take me away to _____

_____

_____

Brands & Scents

Bubble bath _____

_____

Baby powder _____

_____

Cologne/perfume _____

_____

Hair products_____

_____

_____

Cosmetics _____

_____

_____

Skin care _____

_____

_____

Nail polish _____Colors _____

Pamper me

My hair salon _____

phone # _____

preferred attendant _____

My preferred place for a:

Manicure/pedicure: _____

phone # _____

preferred attendant _____

Massage: _____

phone # _____

preferred attendant _____

Facial: _____

phone # _____

preferred attendant _____

Foods I Crave

When I'm...

happy _____

_____

_____

sad _____

_____

_____

want to celebrate _____

_____

_____

famished _____

_____

_____

anxious _____

_____

_____

Restaurants

My favorite(s) _____

_____

_____

_____

What I look for in a good restaurant _____

_____

_____

_____

A romantic restaurant is one that _____

_____

_____

_____

A fun restaurant is _____

_____

_____

_____

My Favorite Foods

Breakfast _____

Breakfast roll _____

Lunch _____

Sandwich _____

Drink _____

Appetizer _____

Dinner _____

Vegetable _____

Snack/nosh _____

Dessert _____

Candy _____

Ice cream _____

Favorite Foods (cont.)

Cake _____

Fruit _____

Nut _____

Meat _____

Fish_____

Coffee _____

Tea _____

Treat _____

Foods I will never consider eating, ever! _____

_____

_____

_____

_____

"I hate champagne more than anything
in the world, next to Seven-Up."
— *Elaine Dundy*

Notes

_____

_____

_____

_____

_____

_____

_____

_____

_____

_____

_____

_____

_____

_____

_____

_____

_____

"When love and skill work together,
expect a masterpiece."
— *John Ruskin*

Let's Party!

On the spur of the moment:

What? _____

Where? _____

With whom? _____

A week's notice:

What? _____

Where? _____

With whom? _____

A big event:

What? _____

Where? _____

With whom? _____

It doesn't take money to _____

_____

_____

_____

_____

Notes

_____

_____

_____

_____

_____

_____

_____

_____

_____

_____

_____

_____

_____

_____

_____

_____

"To love is to place our happiness
in the happiness of another."
— _Gottfried Wilhelm von Leibniz_

Surprise me!

Here is how I feel about surprises: _____

_____

_____

_____

_____

Little surprises to lift me up: _____

_____

_____

_____

_____

If you want to surprise me in a big way: _____

_____

_____

_____

_____

_____

Notes

"Love must be learned, and learned again and again;
there is no end to it."
—*Katherine Ann Porter*

Turn me on

I feel most romantic when _____

_____

I like to wear _____

_____

I like to hear _____

_____

I like to see _____

_____

I like to feel _____

_____

I like to smell _____

_____

I like to be _____

_____

My favorite place to be kissed by you is _____

Notes

_____

_____

_____

_____

_____

_____

_____

_____

_____

_____

_____

_____

_____

_____

_____

"You don't know a woman
until you have had a letter from her."
—*Ada Levenson*

Getting the Message

Here is how I feel about:

Love notes_____

_____

Thank-you notes _____

_____

Letters _____

_____

Getting mail _____

_____

"E" Mail _____

_____

Answering machines/voice mail _____

_____

Fax machines _____

_____

Notes

_____

_____

_____

_____

_____

_____

_____

_____

_____

_____

_____

_____

_____

_____

_____

_____

_____

_____

"We are not the same persons this year as last; nor are those we love.
It is a happy chance if we, changing, continue to love a changed person."
—*W. Somerset Maugham*

Other suggestions

_____

_____

_____

_____

_____

_____

_____

_____

_____

_____

_____

_____

_____

_____

_____

_____

_____

_____

_____

Notes

_____

_____

_____

_____

_____

_____

_____

_____

_____

_____

_____

_____

_____

_____

_____

_____

"For you to ask advice on the rules of love is no better
than to ask advice on the rules of madness."
—*Terence*

Some Private Thoughts

What I adore about you _____

_____

My favorite memory _____

_____

Some day I would _____

_____

If I could change anything in my life_____

_____

My most cherished possession _____

_____

My favorite place of retreat _____

_____

If I had all the time in the world_____

_____

Notes

_____

_____

_____

_____

_____

_____

_____

_____

_____

_____

_____

_____

_____

"Men always want to be a woman's first love.
That is their clumsy vanity.
Women have a more subtle instinct about things:
what they like is to be a man's last romance."
—*Oscar Wilde*

Fantasies

Whether you dream of intimate interludes, exotic get-aways, or a shopping extravaganza, this is the place to speak freely to your partner! Use your imagination.

Notes

_____

_____

_____

_____

_____

_____

_____

_____

_____

_____

_____

_____

_____

_____

_____

"There is a wealth of unexpressed love in the world.
It is one of the chief causes evoked by death;
What might have been said or done, but that was never said or done."
— *Arthur Hopkins*

Personal Wishes

Planning the future together is not always filled with rosy dreams. Here are some thoughts I would like you to be aware of.

If I am ever in the hospital for an extended stay _____

_____

_____

My final wishes include _____

_____

_____

I always wanted to spend eternity _____

_____

_____

Other thoughts on this include _____

_____

_____

_____

_____

_____

Notes

_____

_____

_____

_____

_____

_____

_____

_____

_____

_____

_____

_____

_____

_____

_____

_____

_____

"The remarkable thing about the human mind
is its range of limitations."
— *Celia Green*

More Thoughts

_____

_____

_____

_____

_____

_____

_____

_____

_____

_____

_____

_____

_____

_____

_____

_____

_____

_____

_____

_____

_____

Notes

_____

_____

_____

_____

_____

_____

_____

_____

_____

_____

_____

_____

_____

_____

_____

_____

_____

_____

_____

"Most folks are about as happy as they make up their mind to be."
— _Abraham Lincoln_

Helpful Hints

1. Let your partner know she is special to you every day. Whether it is an unexpected formal gift, or a simple phone call or post-it note on the refrigerator, tell her that she is a special part of your life.

2. Buy several cards at one time for those important days (birthday, anniversary, etc.). Store them in this book for safe keeping and they will always be ready for your when you need them. Take the time to browse while you are in the mood, and choose the cards that remind you of special times you spent with your partner.

3. Mark your personal calendar and send the cards at least a few days in advance. Receiving that birthday card early is a lot more satisfying than receiving it late!

4. Little things mean a lot. Take care in the smallest gestures. When writing a note, use nice paper and a pen that doesn't blot.

5. Make use of the free gift-wrap and other store services that are often offered. Many are environmentally friendly, and it is always nicer to receive a present in a box with a bow, rather than in the store's bag.

Helpful Hints (cont.)

6. Sit down with your calendar and make time to remember your partner, whether you mail her a note, set up a regular date with a sitter for the kids, or plan a get-away weekend.

7. Other than holidays, there are times when your partner will most appreciate your attentiveness: when she's tired or stressed, when she's coming home from a business trip, preparing for an important meeting, or after a hard day at work or at home (children can be more draining than a board meeting!). Your actions show that she's a priority in your life, and that feels good.

8. Clip out ideas as you come across them, and store them in this book (advertisements, articles, theater reviews, catalog pages, etc.). You never know when you'll wish you had a good suggestion.

9. You can never do too much to make someone in your life know what they mean to you. Time is fleeting; don't put off what you can do today.

Appreciation is easy

The following pages contain certificates that can be copied directly out of this book onto beautiful paper at your local photocopy center. Use one of the certificate ideas provided, or use one of the blank ones to create your own special coupon for your partner.

It is always nice to receive a gift like this, enclosed in a meaningful card or nicely-wrapped box. Your partner will enjoy your gift knowing that you want him to enjoy it!

Certificate

*The bearer of this certificate
is entitled to:*

Breakfast
in Bed

To be redeemed: _____

Certificate

*The bearer of this certificate
is entitled to:*

A
Perfect
Picnic

To be redeemed: _____

Certificate

*The bearer of this certificate
is entitled to:*

A
Romantic
Lunch

To be redeemed: _____

Certificate

The bearer of this certificate is entitled to:

A Hot
&
Bubbly Bath

(Candlelight optional)

To be redeemed: _____

Certificate

*The bearer of this certificate
is entitled to:*

An Evening
on the Town

To be redeemed: _____

Certificate

*The bearer of this certificate
is entitled to:*

A Night
Together
Without
Interruption

To be redeemed: _____

Certificate

*The bearer of this certificate
is entitled to:*

A Night of
Stargazing

To be redeemed: _____

Certificate

*The bearer of this certificate
is entitled to:*

Beverage of your choice, with wonderful conversation in front of a roaring fire.

To be redeemed: _____

Certificate

*The bearer of this certificate
is entitled to:*

Time alone,
all by yourself...
An entire day
or evening to spend
any way you wish.

To be redeemed: _____

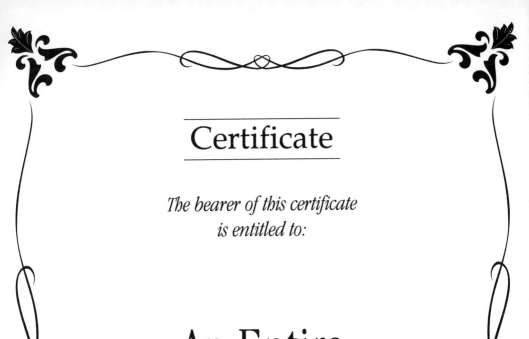

Certificate

*The bearer of this certificate
is entitled to:*

An Entire
Day Together

Your choice of activities!

To be redeemed: _____

Certificate

*The bearer of this certificate
is entitled to:*

To be redeemed: _____

Certificate

The bearer of this certificate
is entitled to:

To be redeemed: _____

People change, and times change. If you have any suggestions

for future additions to this book, or any comments, we would

like to hear from you!

Please direct your correspondence to:

All About Her
c/o The Beverly Clark Collection
1120 Mark Avenue
Carpinteria, CA 93013

Now that she has told you "All About Her," let her

know your own thoughts and ideas with our compan-

ion edition to this book, "All About Him." Look for

both books at your local retailer or contact us at:

The Beverly Clark Collection
1120 Mark Avenue
Carpinteria, CA 93013
(800) 888-6866